2016 GREATEST
POP & MOVIE HITS

ARRANGED BY
ALBERT MENDOZA

CONTENTS

Produced by
Alfred Music
P.O. Box 10003
Van Nuys, CA 91410-0003
alfred.com

D1597031

Printed in USA.

ISBN-10: 1-4706-3346-9
ISBN-13: 978-1-4706-3346-2

Skyscrapers: © iStockphoto.com / gyn9038

ALL I ASK

Words and Music by Chris Brown,
Bruno Mars, Adele Adkins and Philip Lawrence
Arr. Albert Mendoza

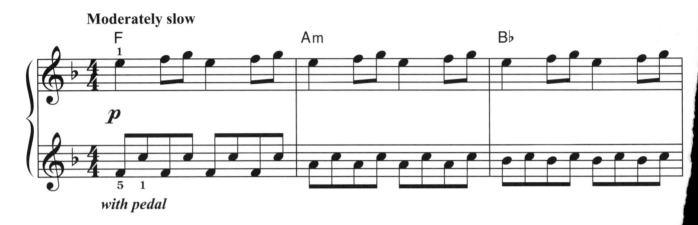

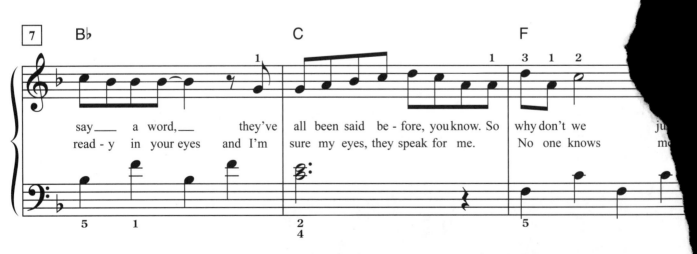

3

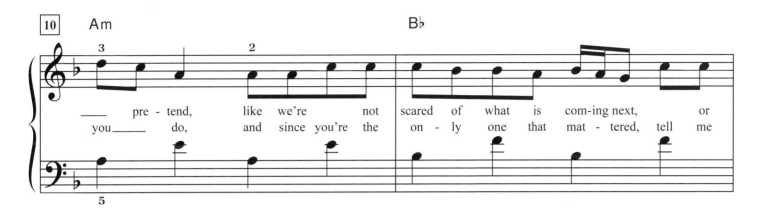

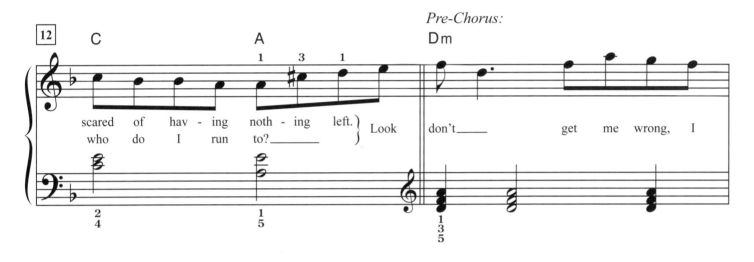

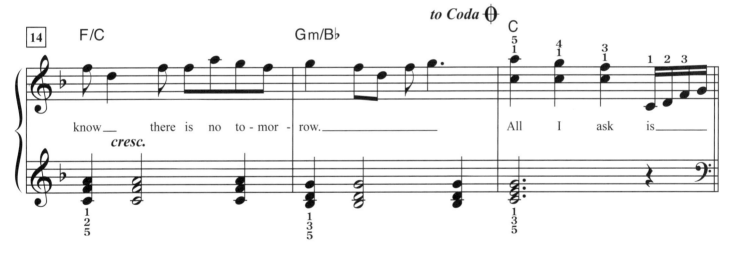

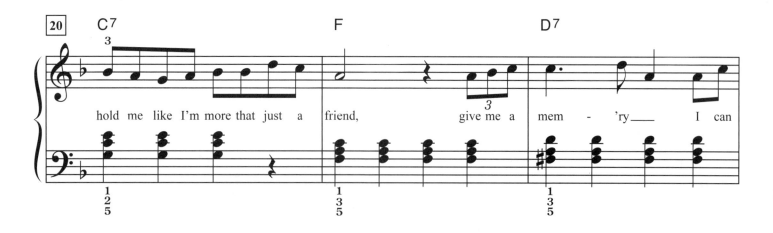

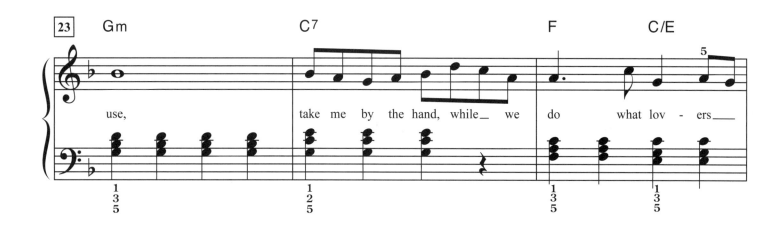

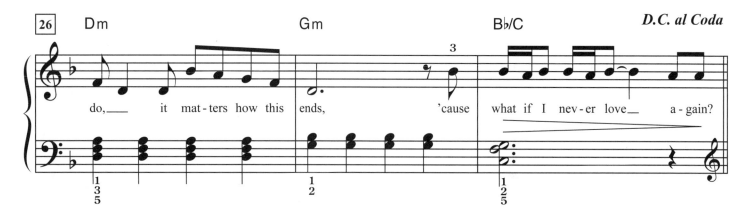

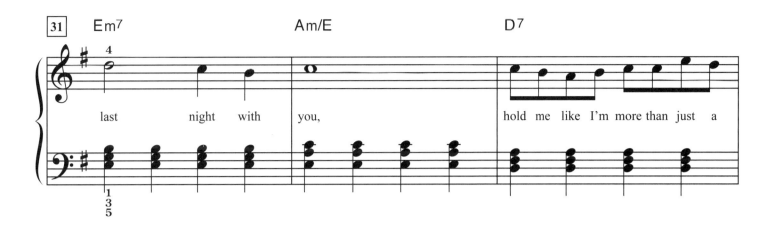

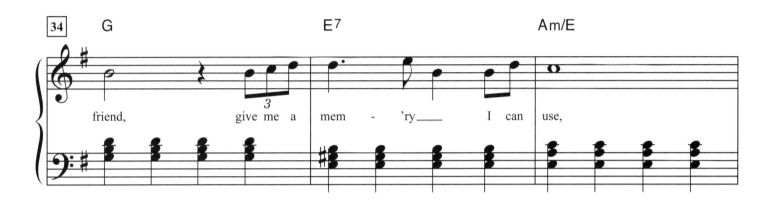

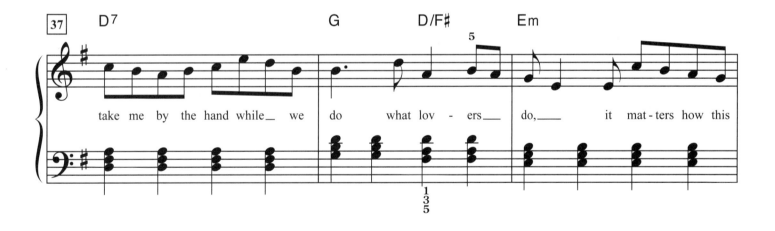

BUNDLE OF JOY

(from *Inside Out*)

Words and Music by Michael Giacchino
Arr. Albert Mendoza

8

BRIGHT

Words and Music by Graham Sierota, Jamie Sierota,
Noah Sierota, Sydney Sierota, Jeffery Sierota and Maureen McDonald
Arr. Albert Mendoza

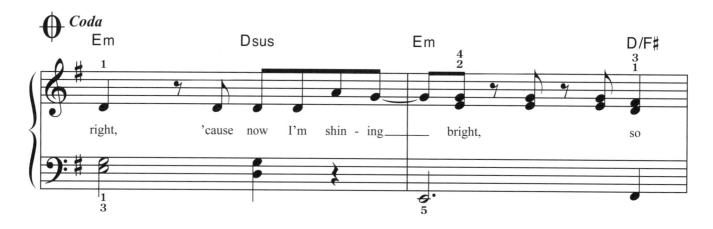

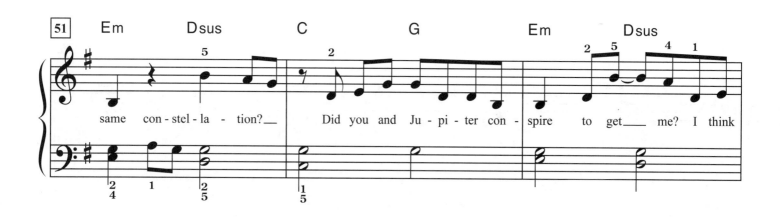

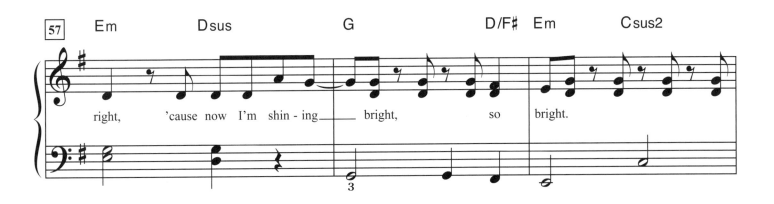

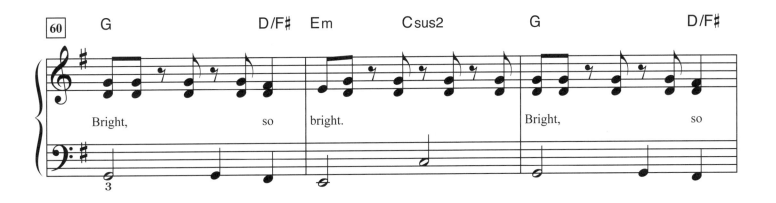

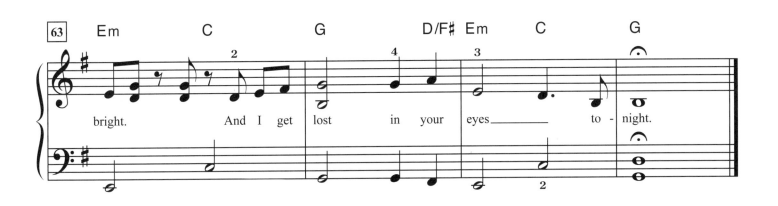

CAN'T FEEL MY FACE

Words and Music by Ali Payami, Savan Kotecha,
Max Martin, Abel Tesfaye and Peter Svensson
Arr. Albert Mendoza

Pre-Chorus:

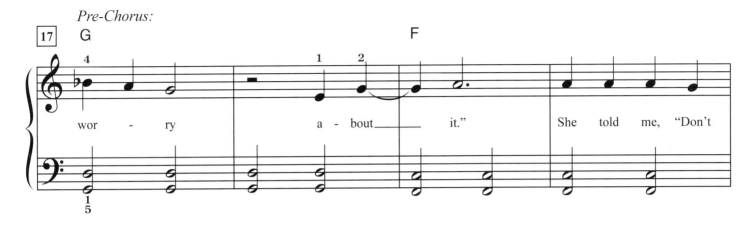

wor - ry a - bout____ it." She told me, "Don't

wor - ry____ no more."____ We both know we

can't____ go with - out____ it. She told me, "You'll

nev - er be in love." Oh, oh, ooh.

cresc.

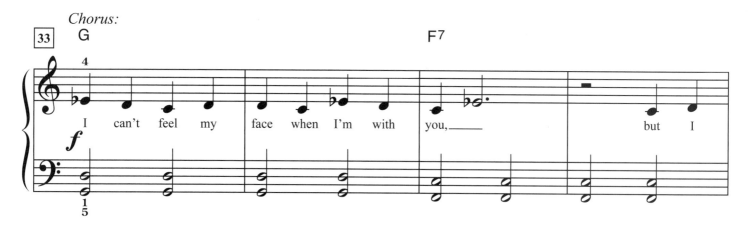

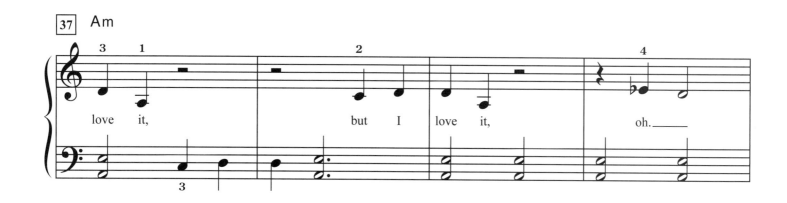

CHEERLEADER

Words and Music by Mark Bradford, Ryan Dillon,
Sly Dunbar, Omar Pasley and Clifton Dillon
Arr. Albert Mendoza

CENTURIES

Words and Music by Suzanne Vega, Justin Tranter,
Raja Kumari, Jonathan Rotem, Michael Fonesca,
Andrew Hurley, Patrick Stumph, Pete Wentz and Joseph Trohman
Arr. Albert Mendoza

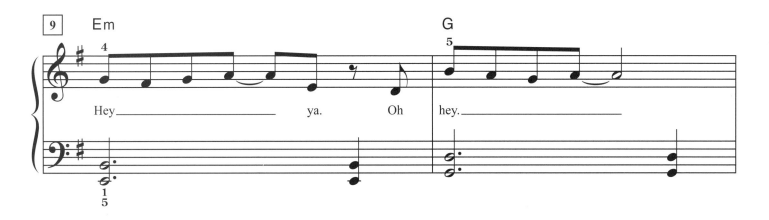

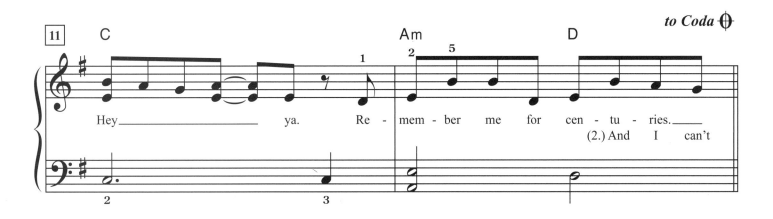

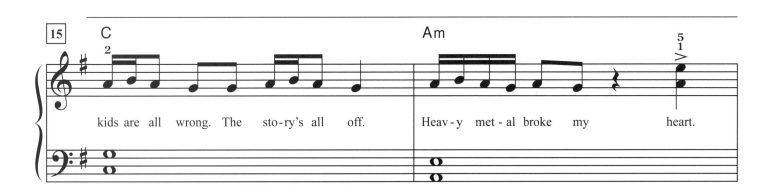

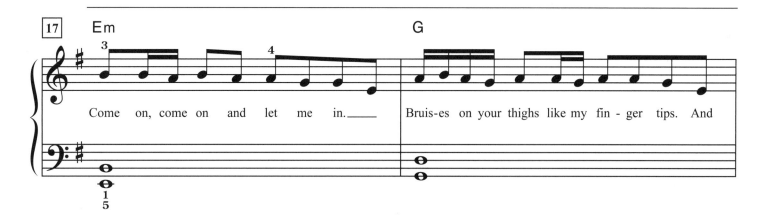

17 Em ... G

Come on, come on and let me in.____ Bruis-es on your thighs like my fin - ger tips. And

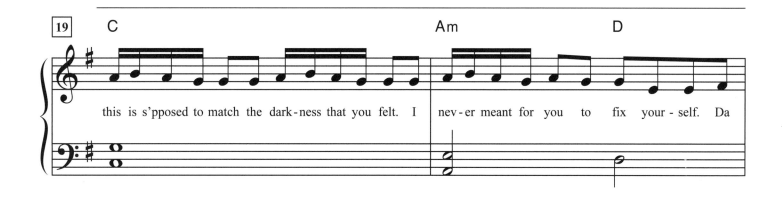

19 C ... Am ... D

this is s'pposed to match the dark-ness that you felt. I nev - er meant for you to fix your - self. Da

21 N.C.

da da da da da____ da da da da da da da da____ da. Some

f

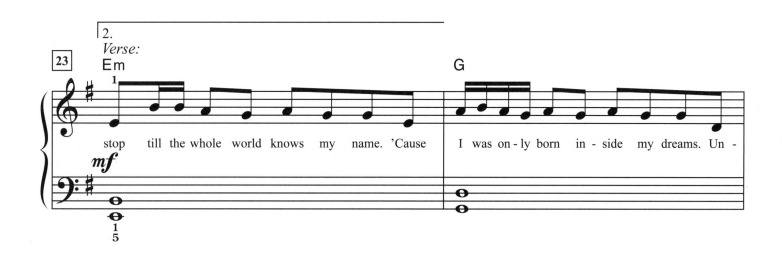

2.
Verse:

23 Em ... G

stop till the whole world knows my name. 'Cause I was on - ly born in - side my dreams. Un -

mf

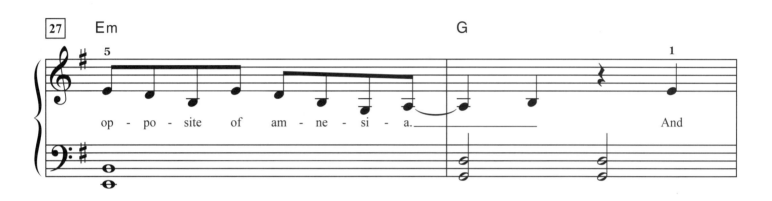

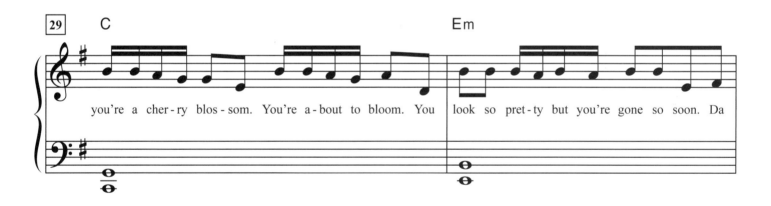

24

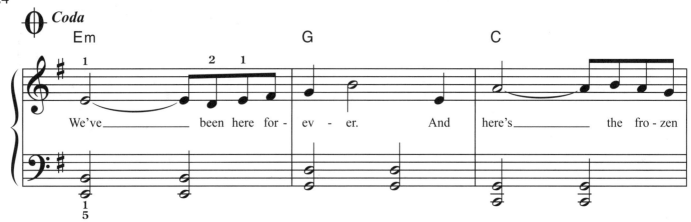

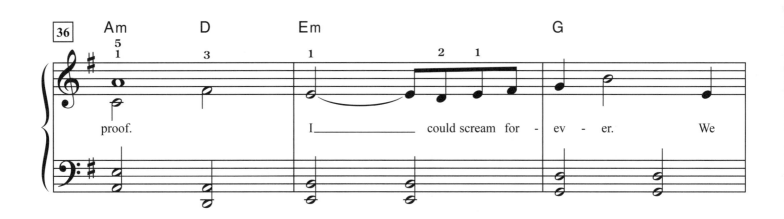

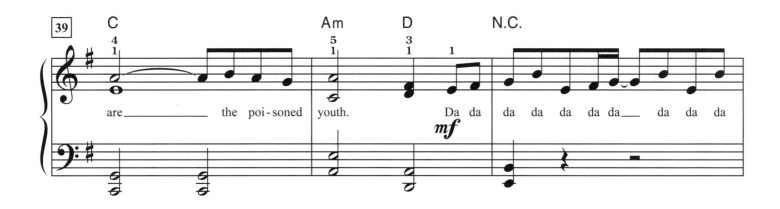

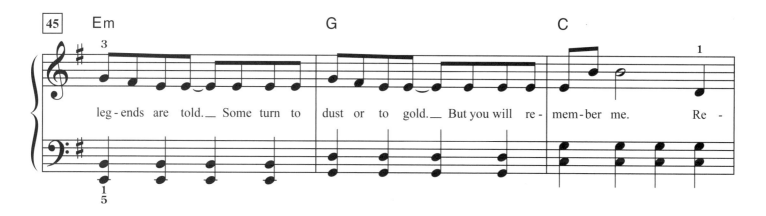

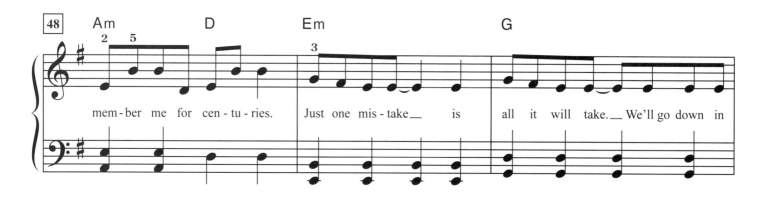

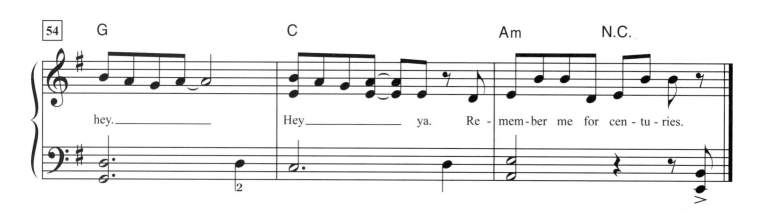

COOL FOR THE SUMMER

Words and Music by
Ali Payami, Savan Kotecha, Max Martin,
Alexander Kronlund and Demitria Lovato
Arr. Albert Mendoza

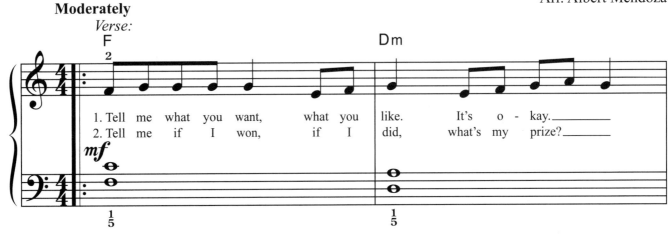

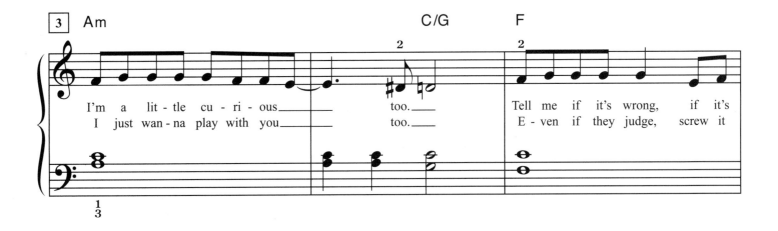

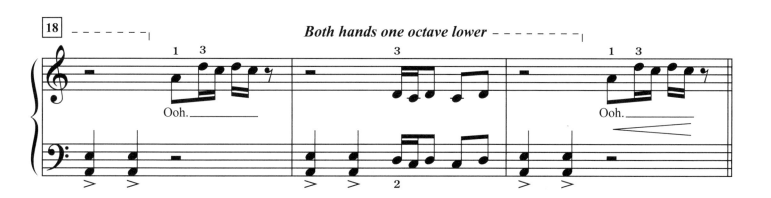

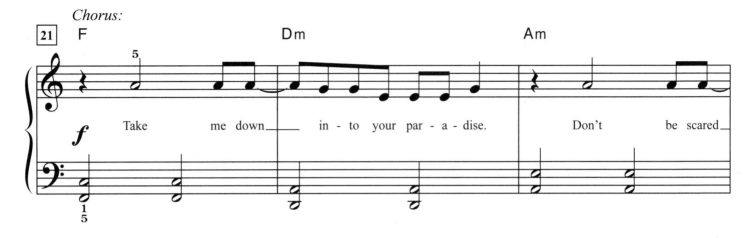

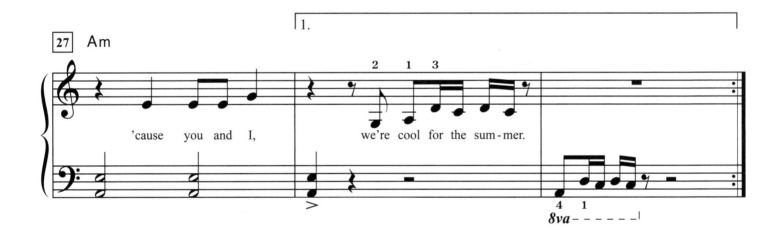

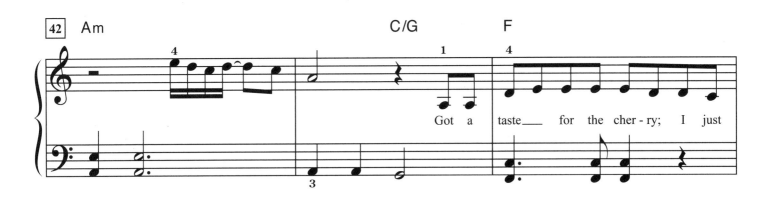

need to take a bite._____

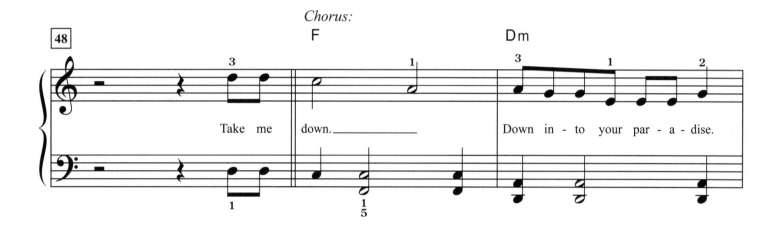

Chorus:

Take me down._____ Down in - to your par - a - dise.

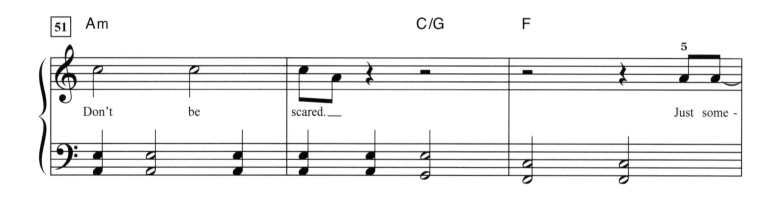

Don't be scared.____ Just some -

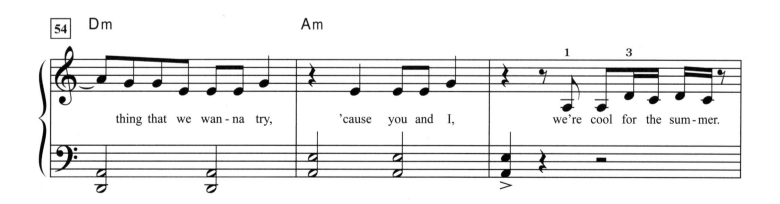

thing that we wan - na try, 'cause you and I, we're cool for the sum - mer.

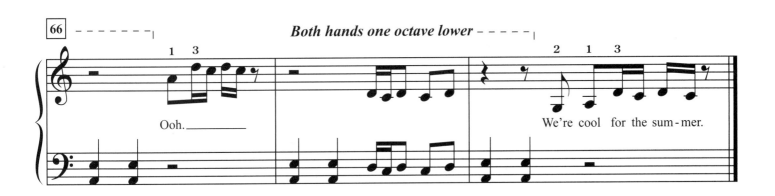

FOCUS

Words and Music by Ilya, Savan Kotecha,
Peter Svensson and Ariana Grande
Arr. Albert Mendoza

Pre-Chorus:

find a light___ in - side our u - ni - verse now.___ Where

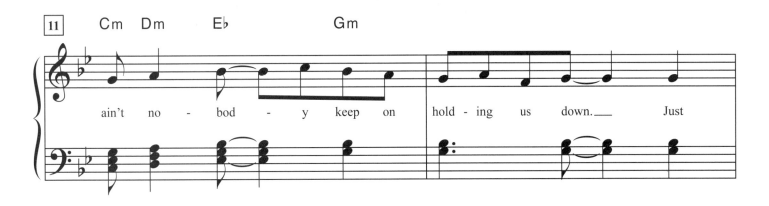

ain't no - bod - y keep on hold - ing us down.___ Just

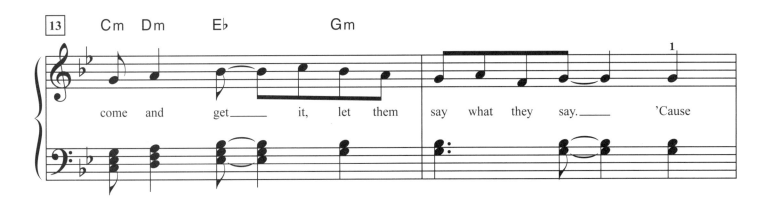

come and get___ it, let them say what they say.___ 'Cause

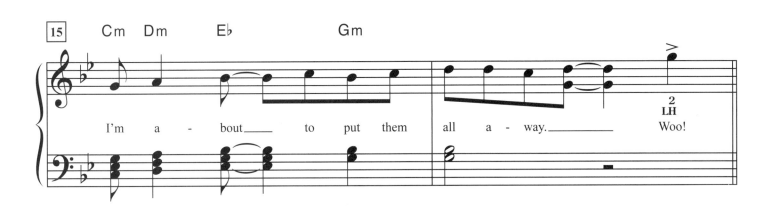

I'm a - bout___ to put them all a - way.___ Woo!

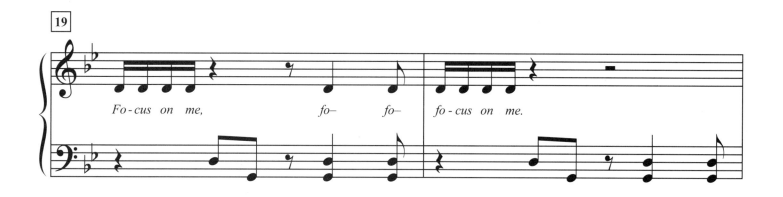

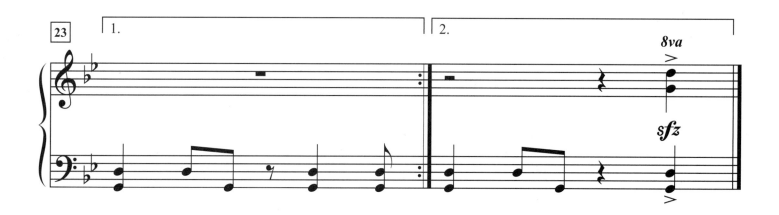

GOOD FOR YOU

Words and Music by Justin Tranter, Nick Monson,
Nolan Lambroza, Julia Michaels and Selena Gomez
Arr. Albert Mendoza

Pre-Chorus:

dress you like, skin-tight, do my | hair up real, real nice, and | syn-co-pate my skin to your heart

Chorus:

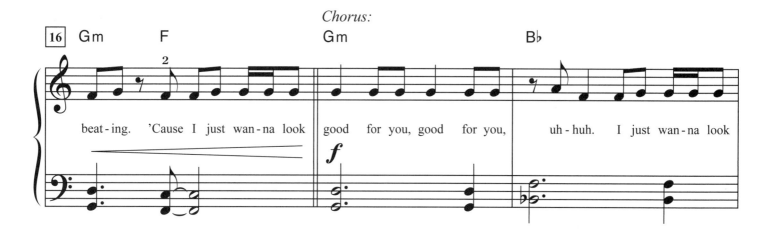

beat-ing. 'Cause I just wan-na look | good for you, good for you, | uh-huh. I just wan-na look

good for you, good for you, | uh-huh. Let me show you how | proud I am to be yours. Leave this

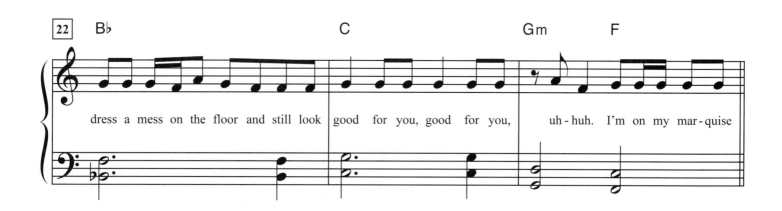

dress a mess on the floor and still look | good for you, good for you, | uh-huh. I'm on my mar-quise

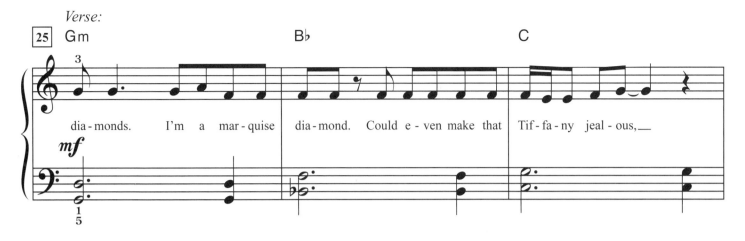

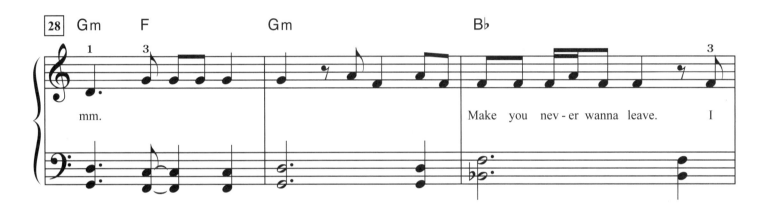

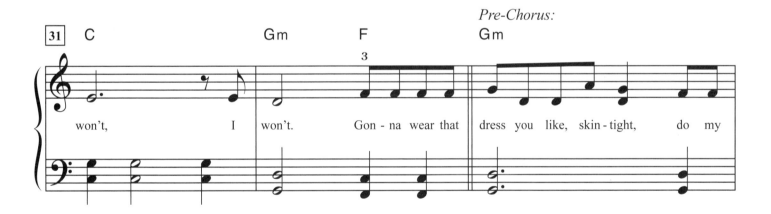

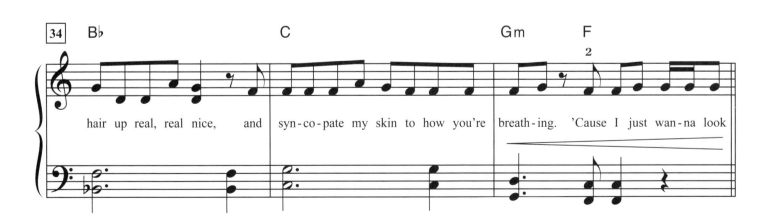

Chorus:

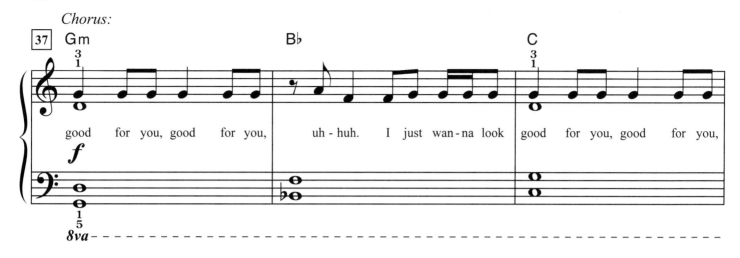

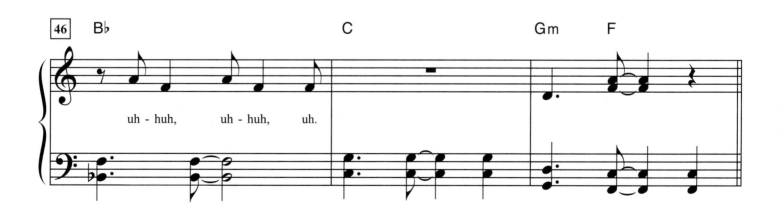

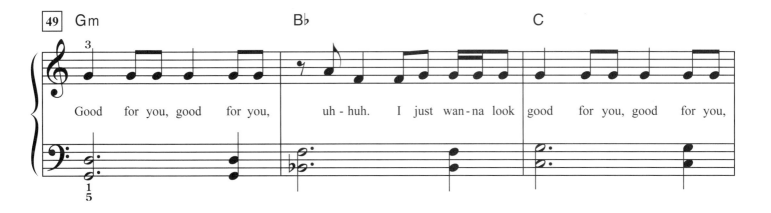

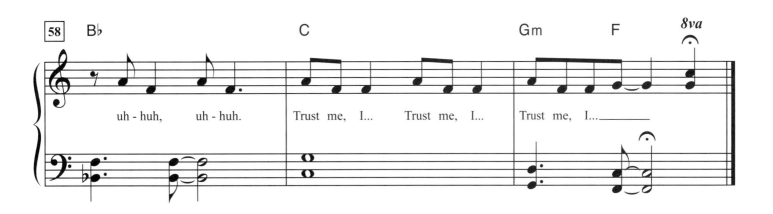

GHOST TOWN

Words and Music by Ali Payami, Tobias Karlsson,
Max Martin, Brandon Lowry and Adam Lambert
Arr. Albert Mendoza

42

HEARTBEAT SONG

Words and Music by Audra Mae, Kelly Clarkson,
Kara Dioguardi and Jason Evigan
Arr. Albert Mendoza

Verse 2:
I, I wasn't even gonna go out
But I never would have had a doubt,
If I'd-a known where I'd be now.
Your hands on my hips,
And my kiss on your lips.
Oh, I could do this for a long time.
(To Chorus:)

LOVE ME LIKE YOU DO

(from *Fifty Shades of Grey*)

Words and Music by Ali Payami, Ilya,
Tove Lo, Max Martin and Savan Kotecha
Arr. Albert Mendoza

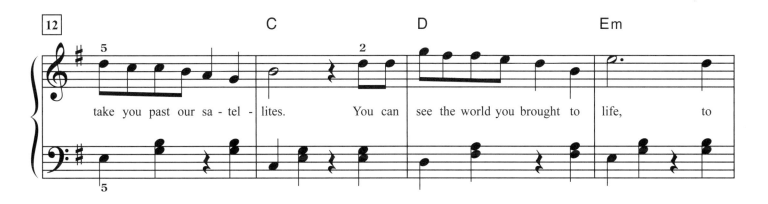

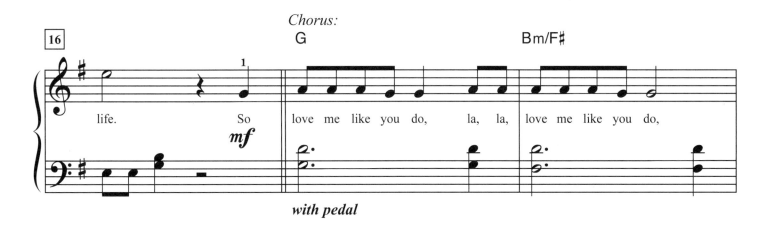

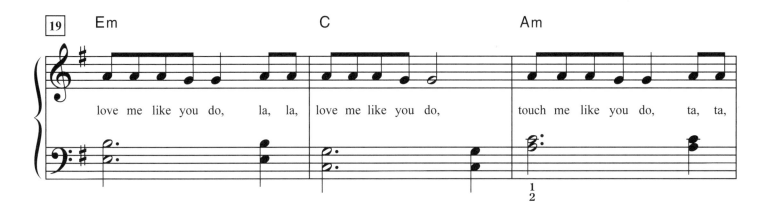

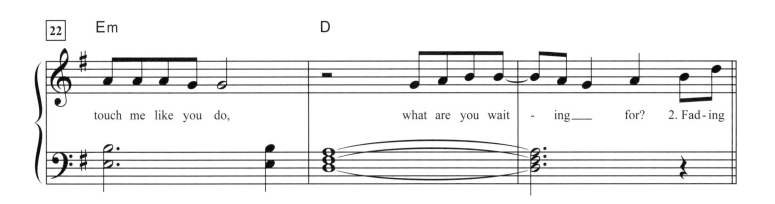

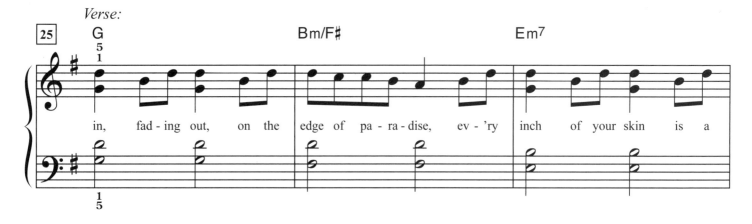

Verse:

25 G Bm/F# Em⁷

in, fad - ing out, on the edge of pa - ra - dise, ev - 'ry inch of your skin is a

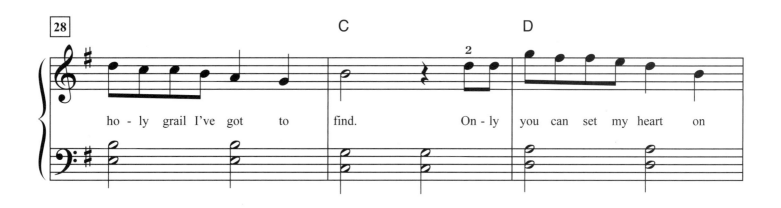

28 C D

ho - ly grail I've got to find. On - ly you can set my heart on

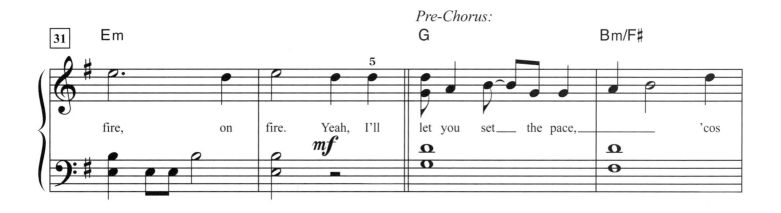

Pre-Chorus:

31 Em G Bm/F#

fire, on fire. Yeah, I'll let you set___ the pace,_____ 'cos

mf

35 Em⁷ C

I'm not think - ing straight,_____ my head spin - ning___ a - round,___

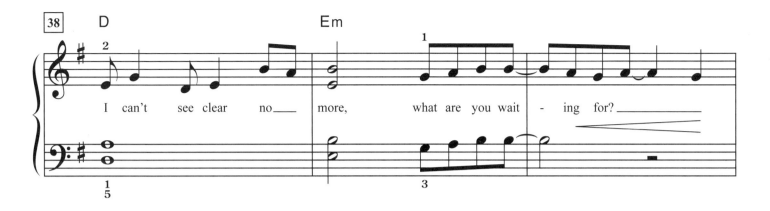

Chorus:

LH one octave lower on repeat

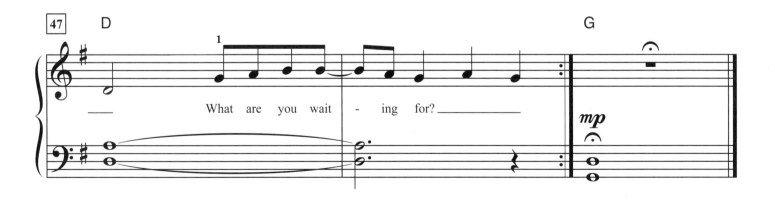

LIKE I'M GONNA LOSE YOU

Words and Music by Justin Weaver,
Caitlyn Smith and Meghan Trainor
Arr. Albert Mendoza

53

MARVIN GAYE

Words and Music by Jacob Luttrell,
Nick Seeley, Charlie Puth and Julie Frost
Arr. Albert Mendoza

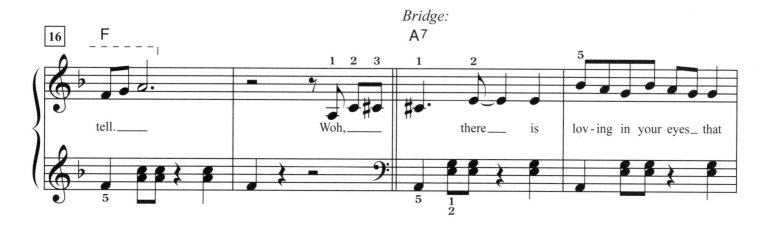

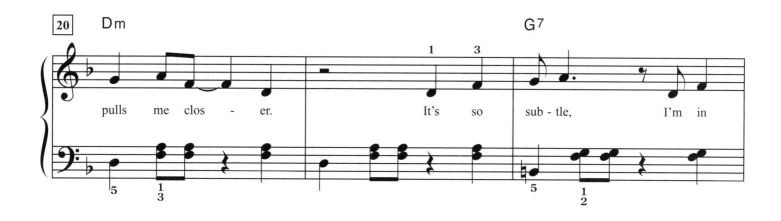

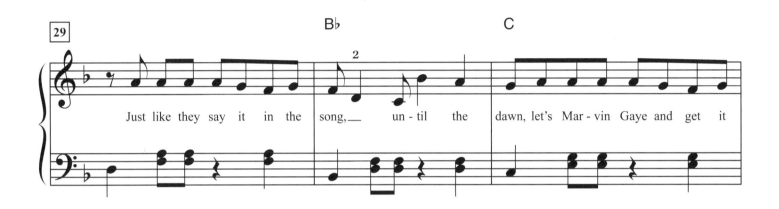

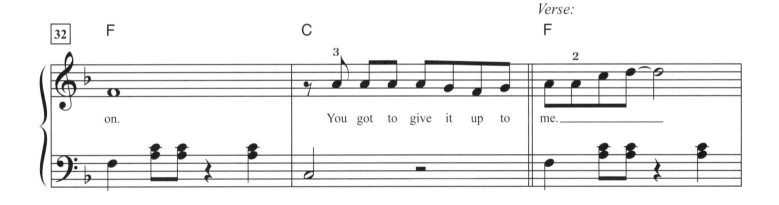

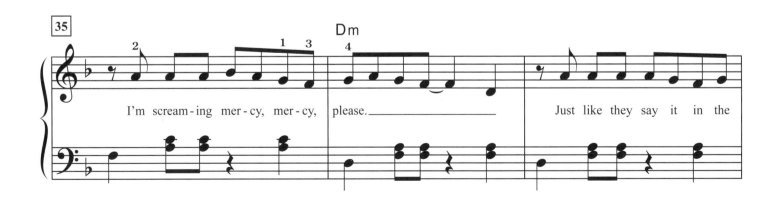

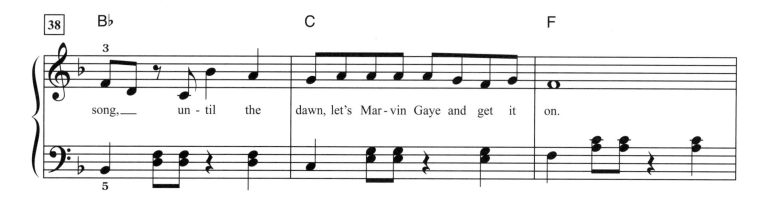

song,___ un-til the dawn, let's Mar-vin Gaye and get it on.

Chorus:

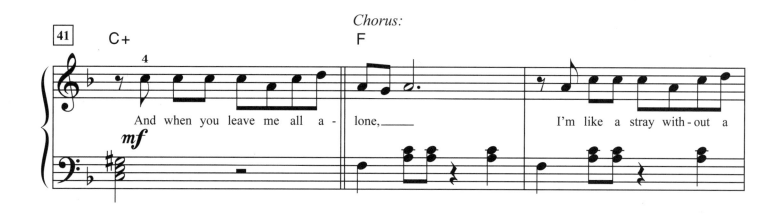

And when you leave me all a-lone,___ I'm like a stray with-out a

home.___ I'm like a dog with-out a bone.___

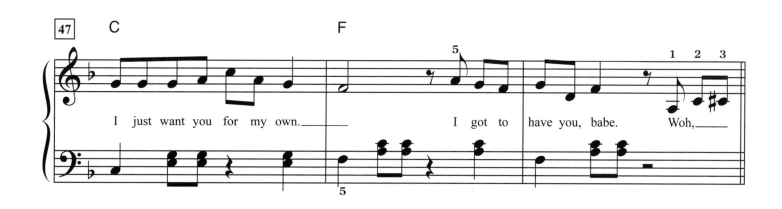

I just want you for my own.___ I got to have you, babe. Woh,___

ME AND MY BROKEN HEART

Words and Music by Wayne Hector, Steve Mac,
Benjamin Levin, Ammar Malik and Rob Thomas
Arr. Albert Mendoza

Quickly
Chorus:

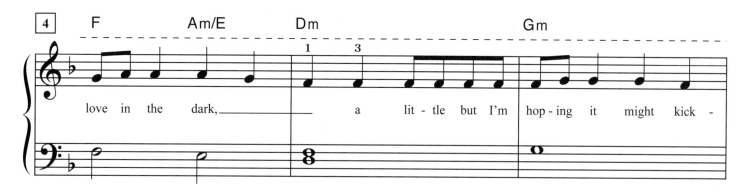

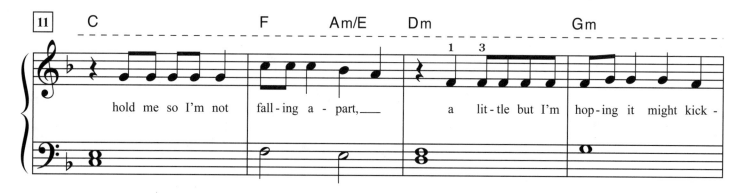

ON MY MIND

Words and Music by Ilya, Savan Kotecha,
Max Martin and Ellie Goulding
Arr. Albert Mendoza

Pre-Chorus:

Chorus:

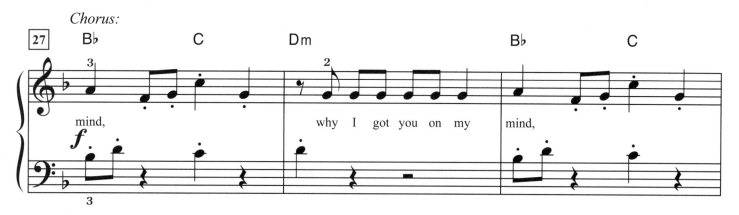

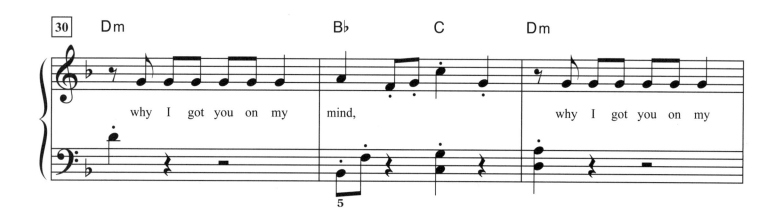

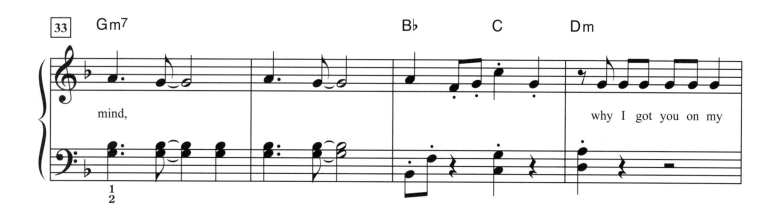

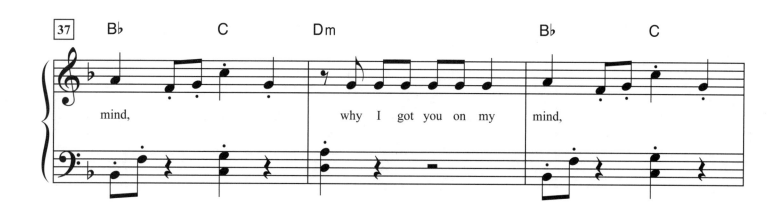

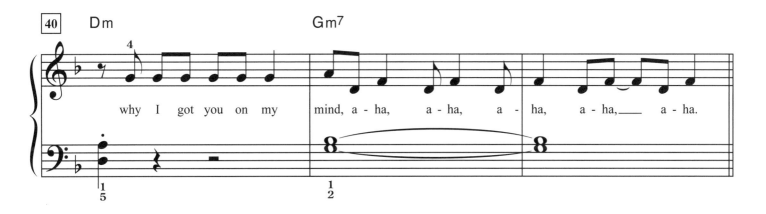

why I got you on my mind, a - ha, a - ha, a - ha, a - ha,___ a - ha.

Verse:

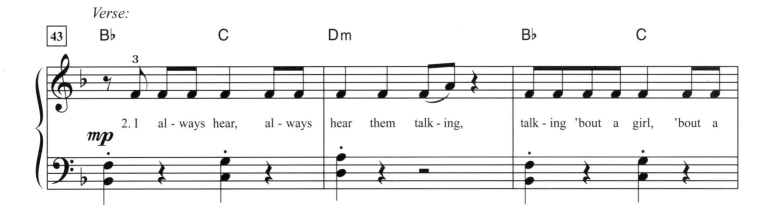

2. I al - ways hear, al - ways hear them talk - ing, talk - ing 'bout a girl, 'bout a

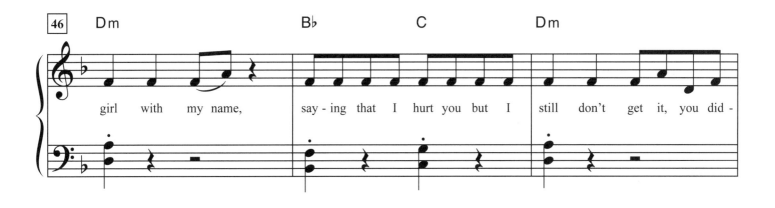

girl with my name, say - ing that I hurt you but I still don't get it, you did -

n't love me,___ no___ not real - ly.___ Wait, I could have real - ly liked you,

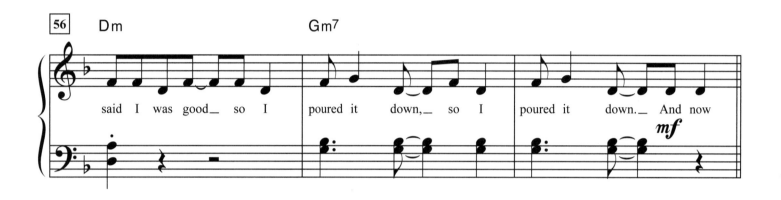

Pre-Chorus:

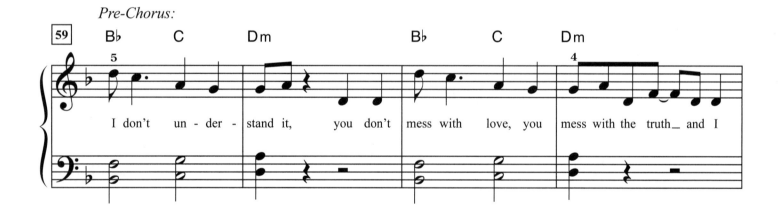

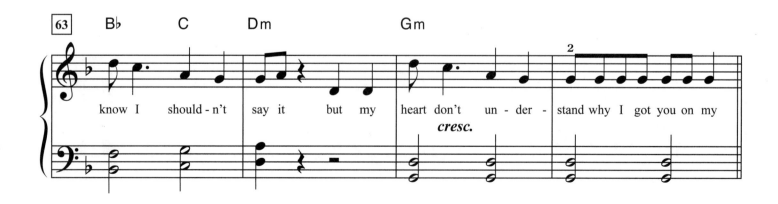

Chorus:

mind, why I got you on my mind, why I got you on my

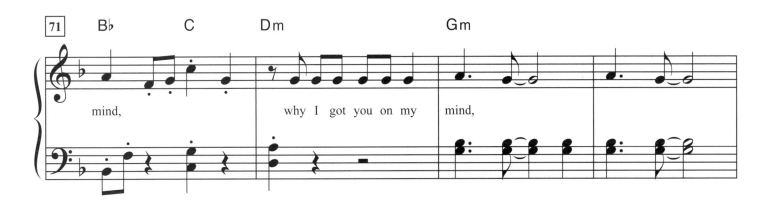

mind, why I got you on my mind,

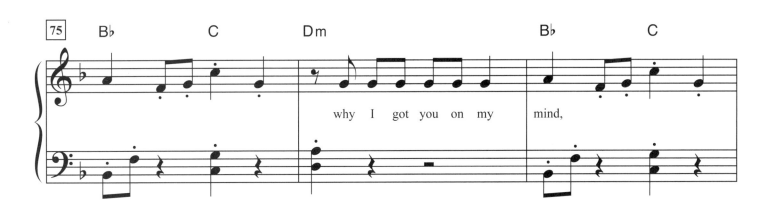

why I got you on my mind,

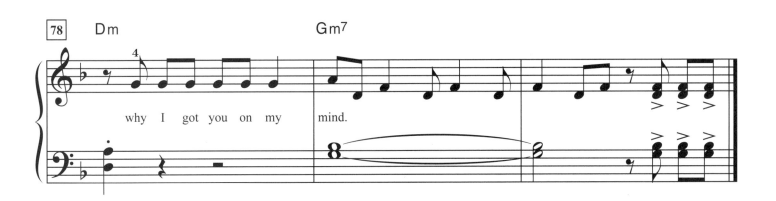

why I got you on my mind.

ONE CALL AWAY

Words and Music by Matthew Prime,
Justin Franks, Charlie Puth, Breyan Isaac,
Maureen McDonald and Shy Carter
Arr. Albert Mendoza

Moderately

Chorus:

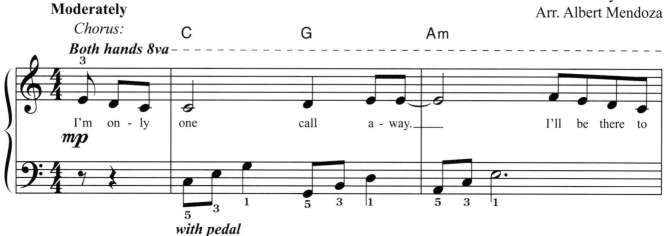

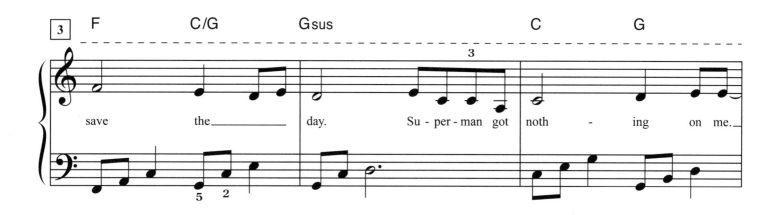

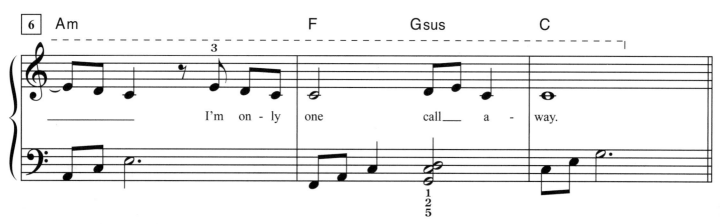

73

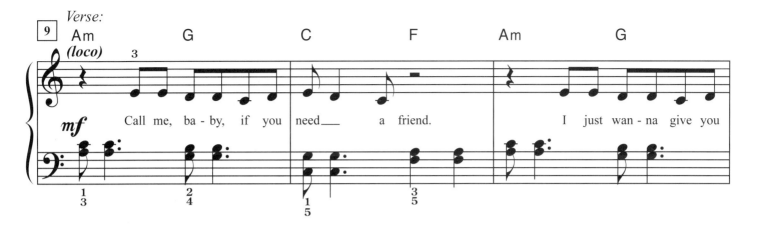

Chorus:

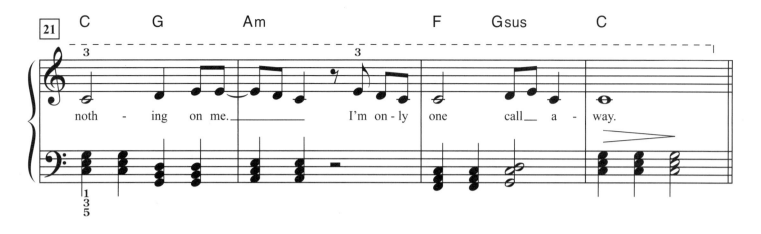

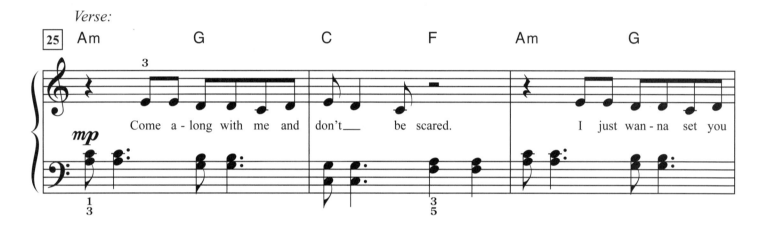

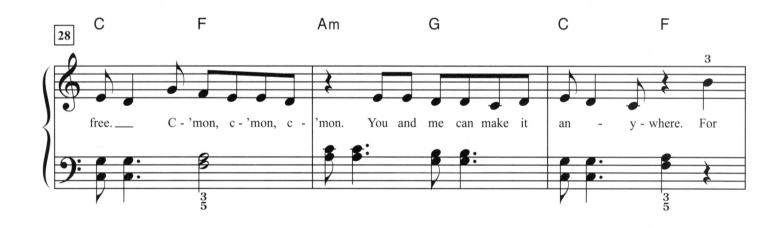

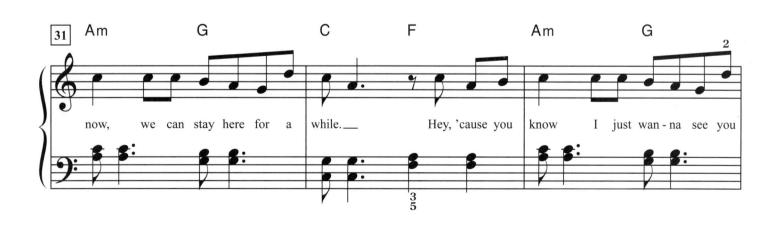

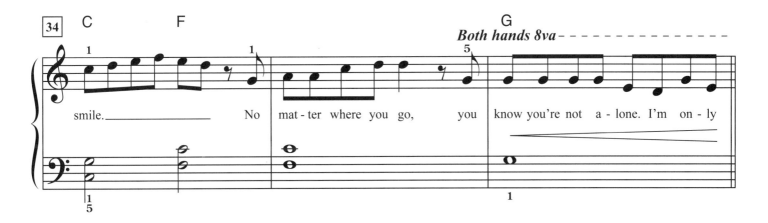

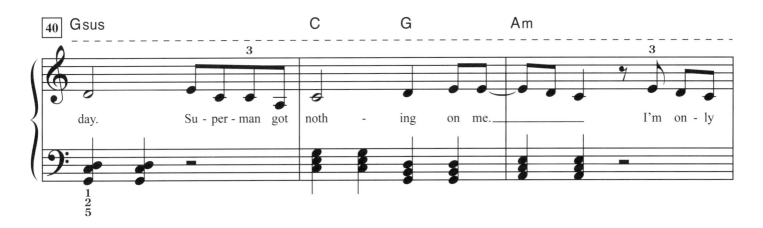

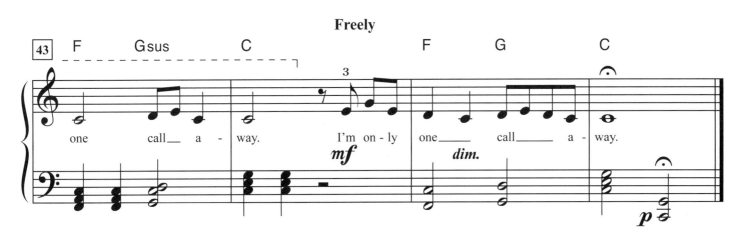

SHUT UP AND DANCE

Words and Music by
Ryan McMahon, Benjamin Berger, Nicholas Petricca,
Sean Waugaman, Kevin Ray and Eli Maiman
Arr. Albert Mendoza

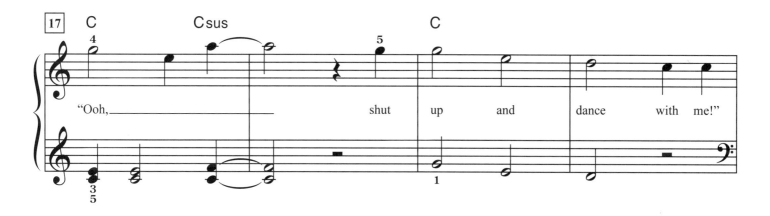

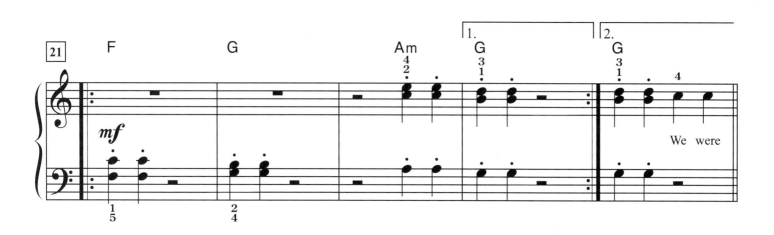

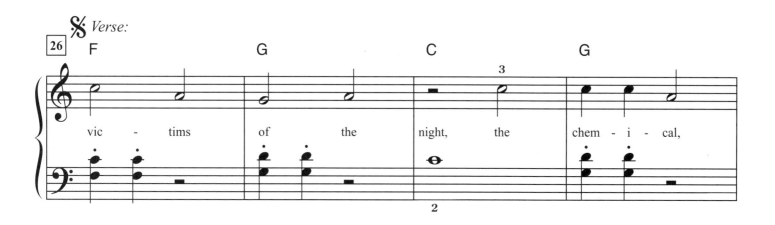

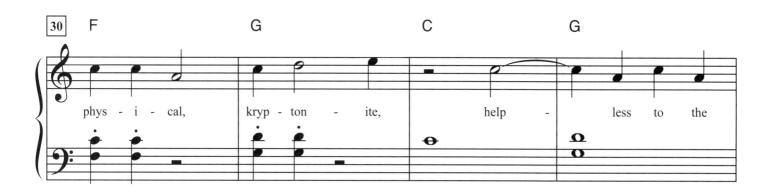

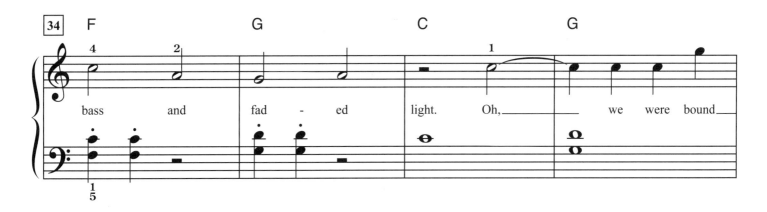

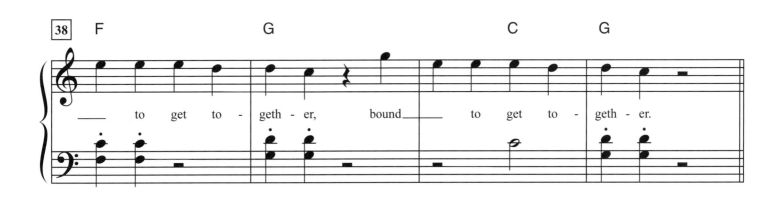

Pre-Chorus:

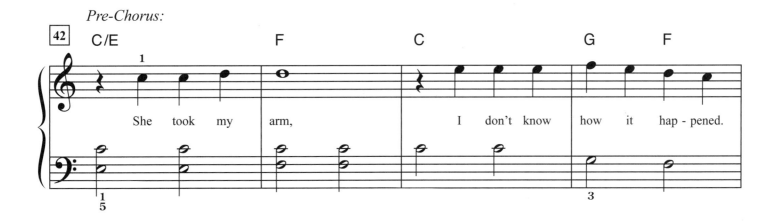

SORRY

Words and Music by
Justin Tranter, Julia Michaels, Justin Bieber,
Sonny Moore and Michael Tucker
Arr. Albert Mendoza

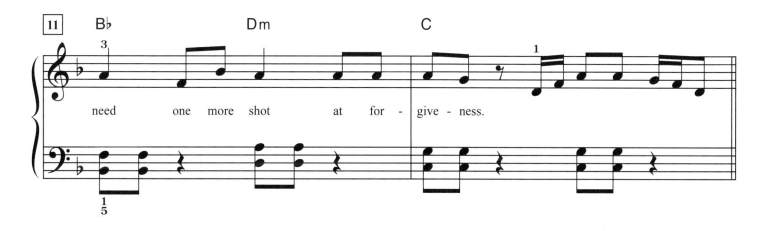

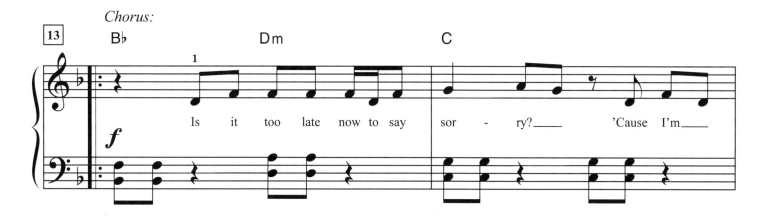

Chorus:

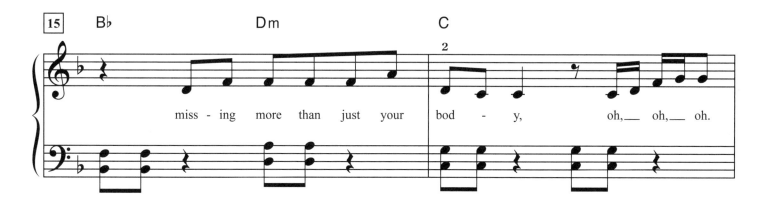

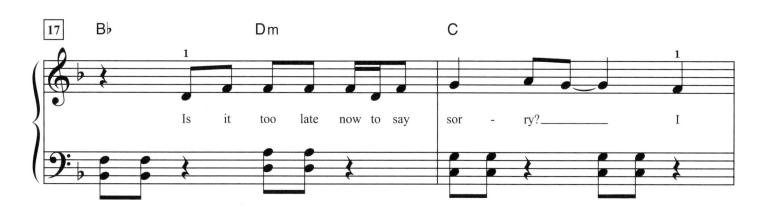

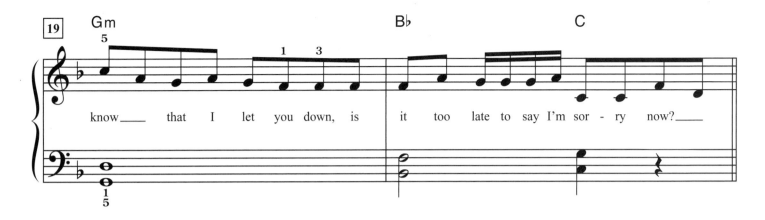

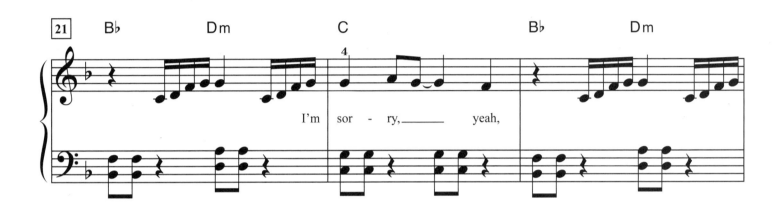

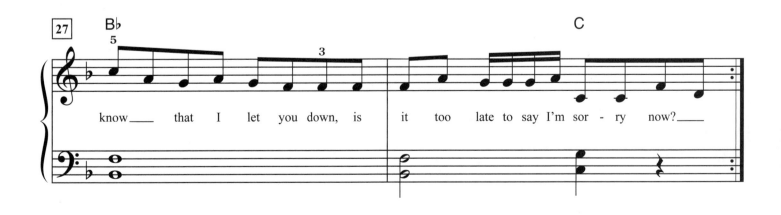

STAR WARS (MAIN THEME)

(from *Star Wars: The Force Awakens*)

Music by **JOHN WILLIAMS**
Arr. Tom Gerou

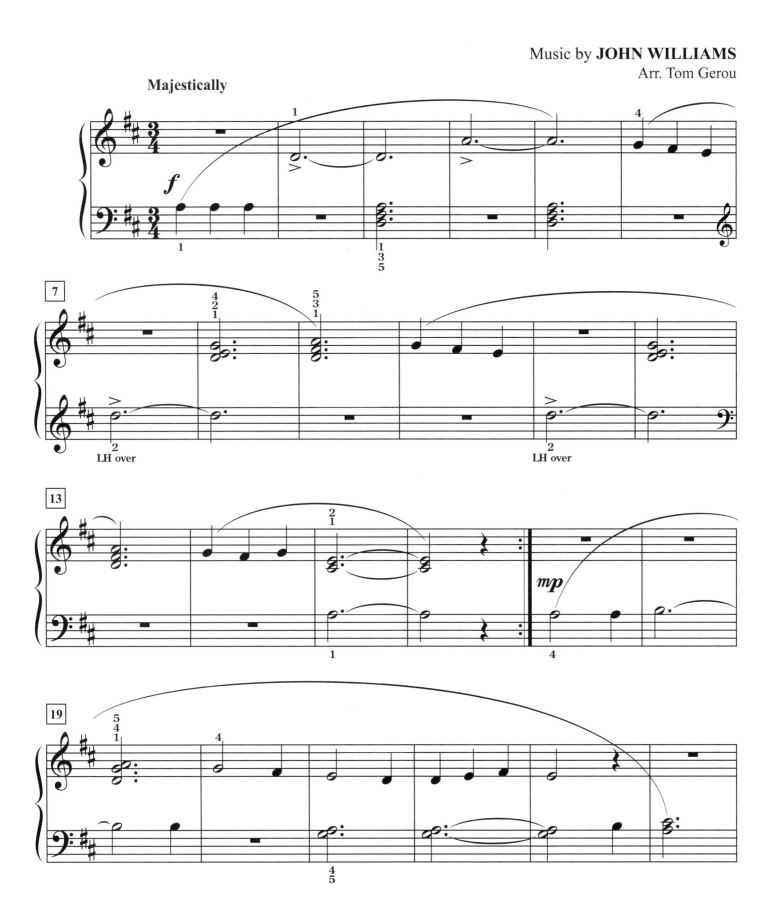

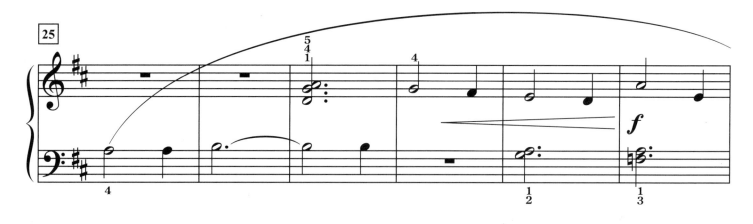

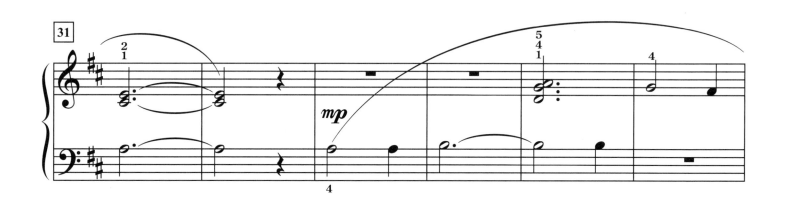

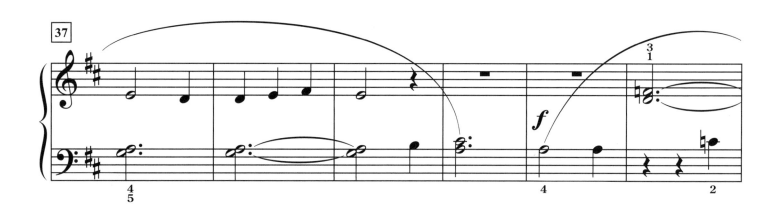

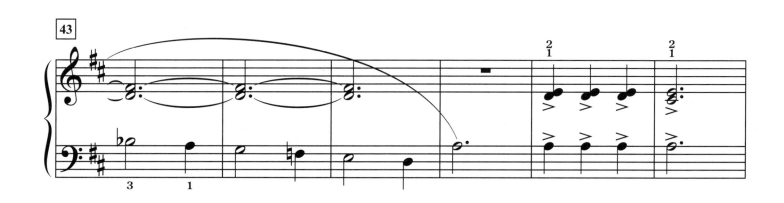

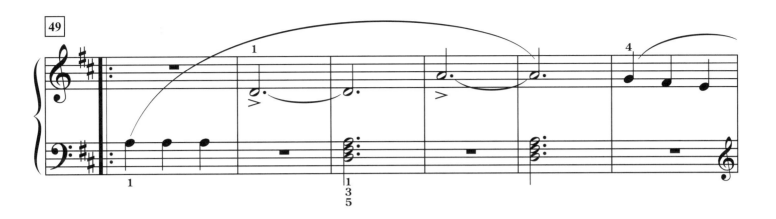

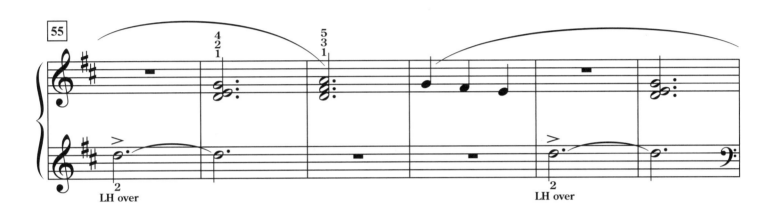

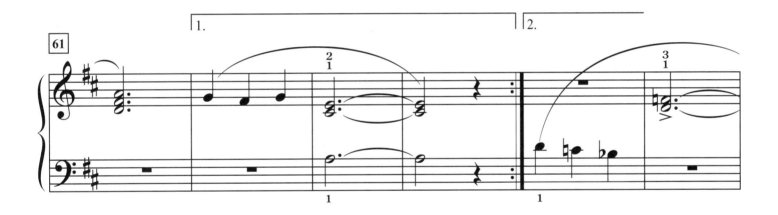

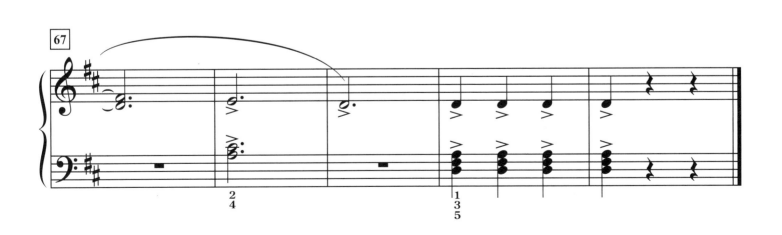

STYLE

Words and Music by Ali Payami,
Johan Schuster, Max Martin and Taylor Swift
Arr. Albert Mendoza

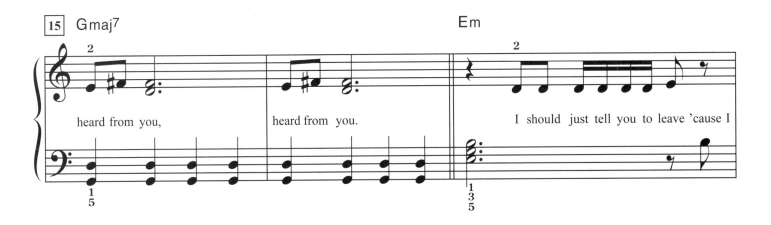

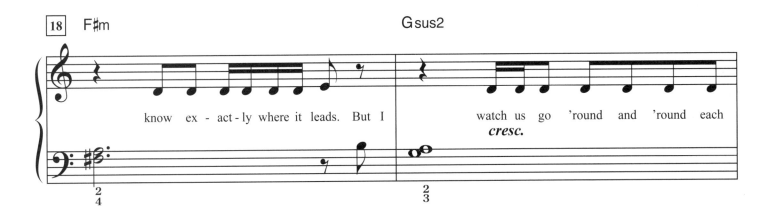

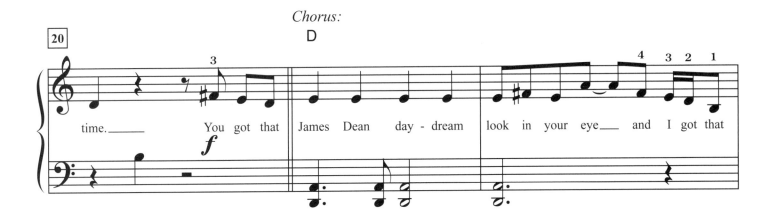

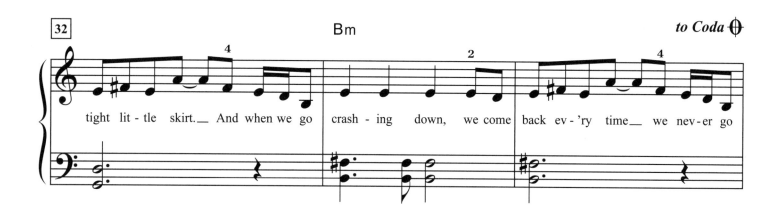

Bridge:

home._____ Just take me home._____ Yeah,_____ just take me

D.S. al Coda

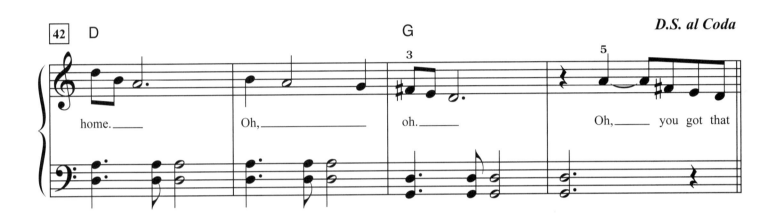

home._____ Oh,_____ oh._____ Oh,_____ you got that

Coda

out of style,_____ we nev-er go out of style._____

Verse 2:
So it goes.
He can't keep his wild eyes on the road.
Take me home.
Lights are off, he's taking off his coat.
I say I heard, oh,
That you been out and about with some other girl.
He says
What you heard is true but I
Can't stop thinking 'bout you and I,
I said I've been there too a few times.
(To Chorus:)

UPTOWN FUNK!

Words and Music by
Bruno Mars, Jeff Bhasker, Philip Lawrence, Devon Gallaspy,
Mark Ronson, Nicholaus Williams, Lonnie Simmons,
Ronnie Wilson, Charles Wilson, Rudolph Taylor and Robert Wilson
Arr. Albert Mendoza

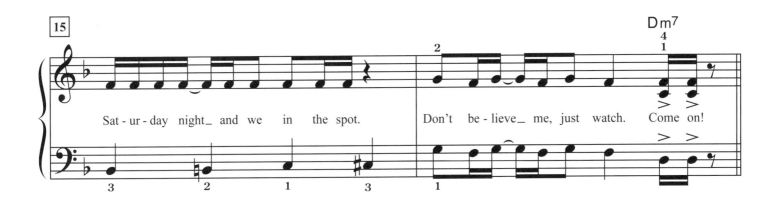

Chorus:

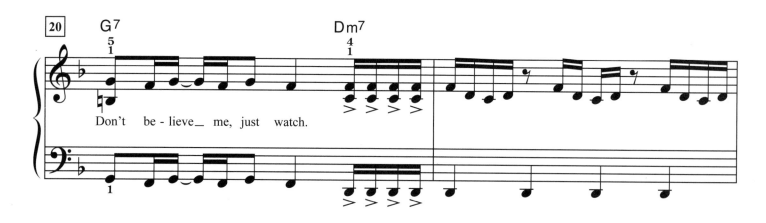

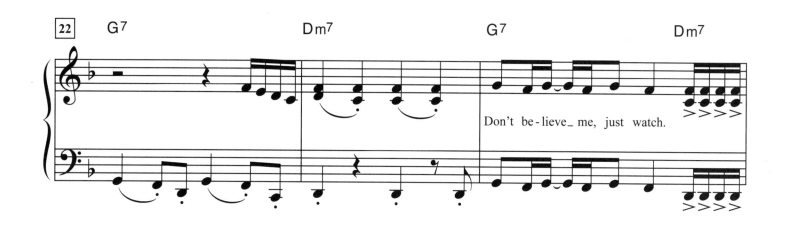

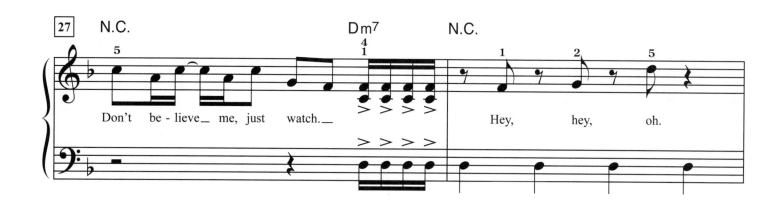

USED TO LOVE YOU

Words and Music by Julia Cavazos, Justin Tranter,
Gwen Stefani, Teal Douville and Jonathan Rotem
Arr. Albert Mendoza

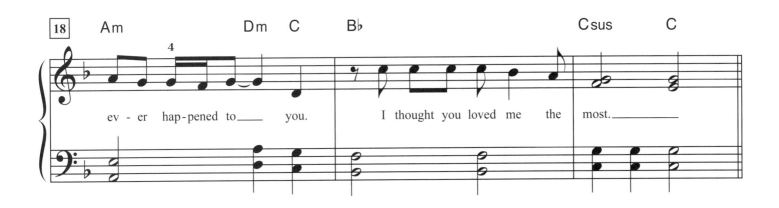

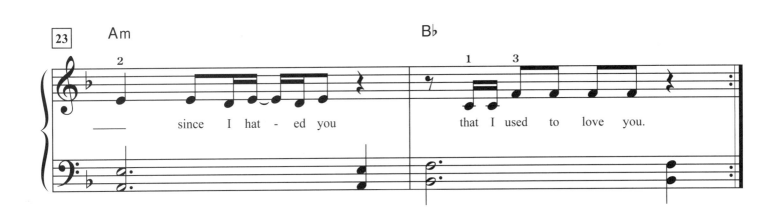

96

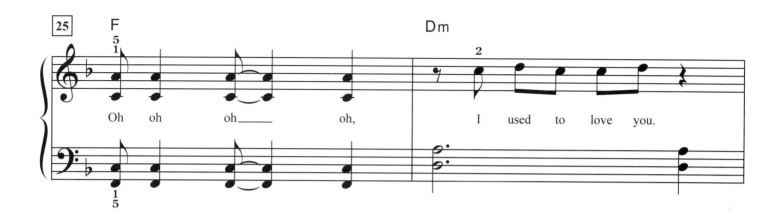

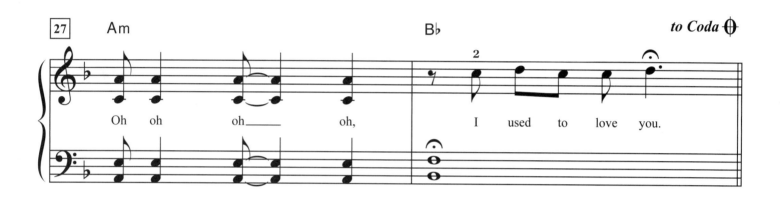

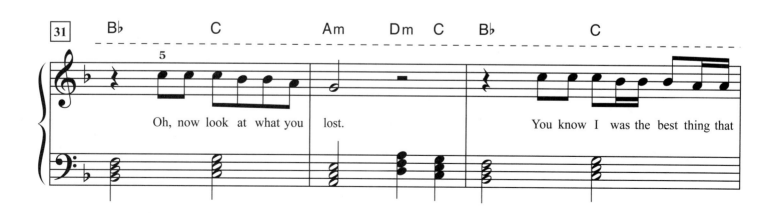

D.S. al Coda

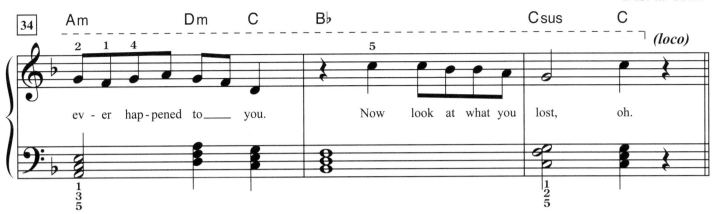

ev - er hap - pened to___ you.   Now   look at what you   lost,   oh.

I don't know why I cry.   No, I don't, I don't, I   don't,   I don't know why I used to

love you,   I don't, I don't, I   don't.   I don't know why I cry.   I don't, I don't, I

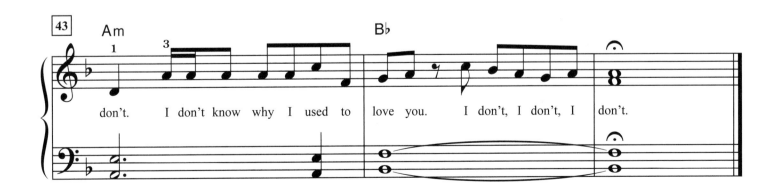

don't.   I don't know why I used to love you.   I don't, I don't, I   don't.

WANT TO WANT ME

Words and Music by Samuel Martin, Ian Kirkpatrick,
Lindy Robbins, Mitch Allan and Jason Desrouleaux
Arr. Albert Mendoza

Steady pop beat

Verse:

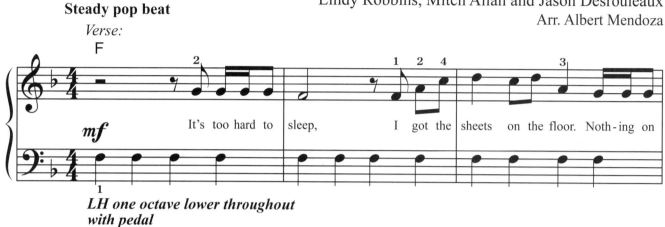

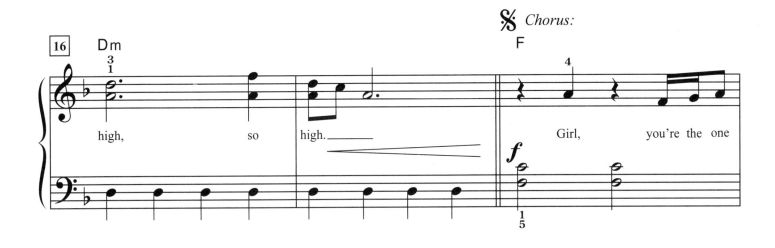

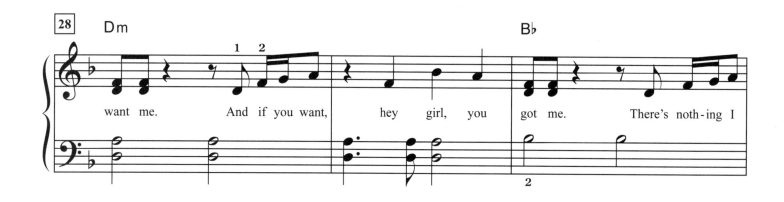

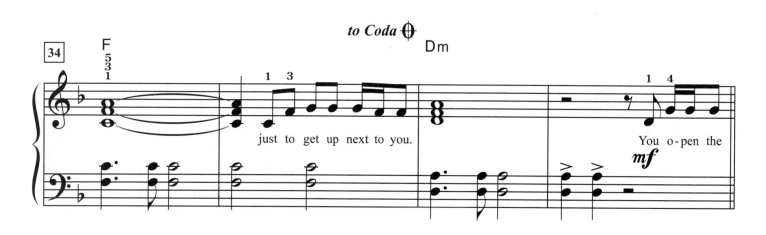

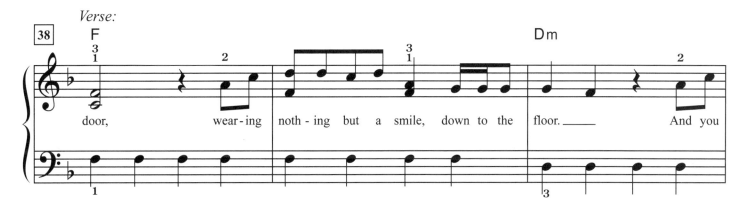

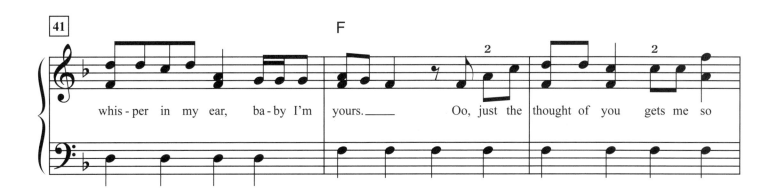

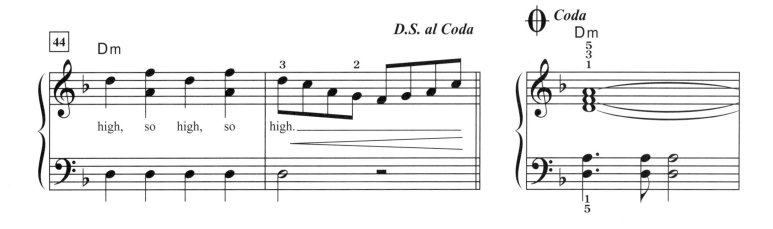

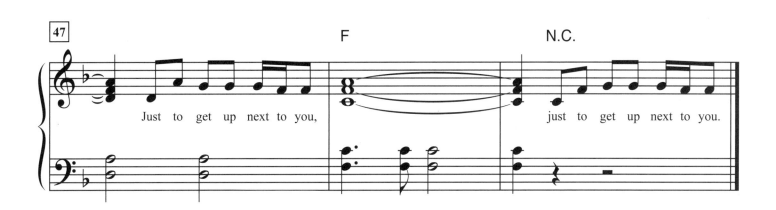

YELLOW FLICKER BEAT

(from *The Hunger Games: Mockingjay, Part 1*)

Words and Music by Mike Dean,
Ella Yelich-O'Connor, Noah Goldstein and Kanye West
Arr. Albert Mendoza

Moderately

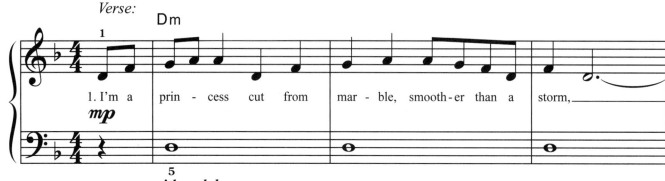

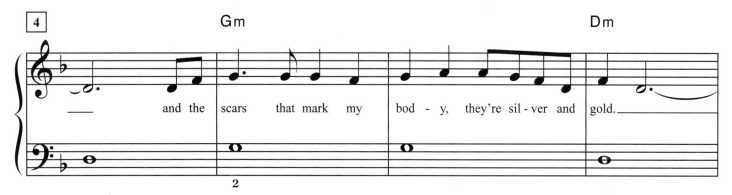

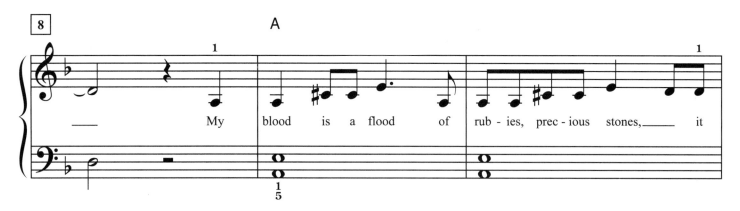

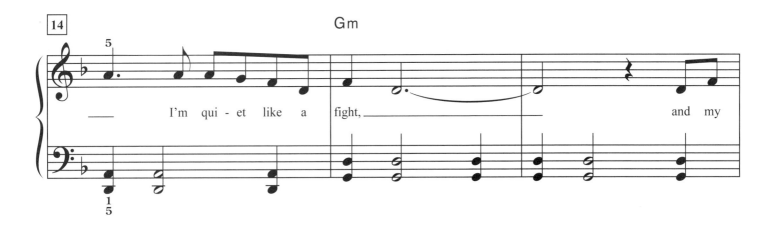

Pre-Chorus:

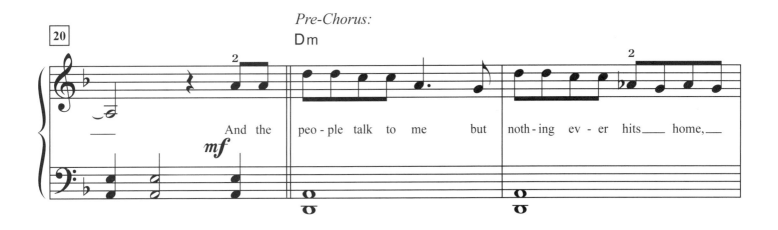

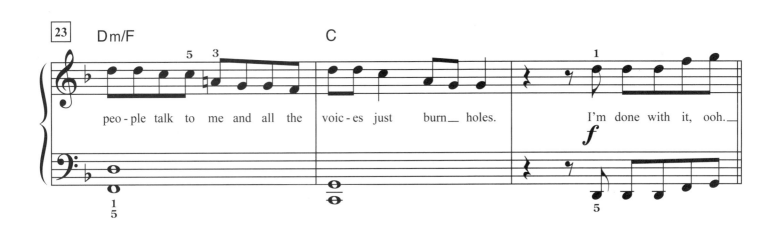

Chorus:

This is the start____ of how it all___ ends, they used to shout my

name, now they whis - per it,___ I'm speed - ing up____ and this is the

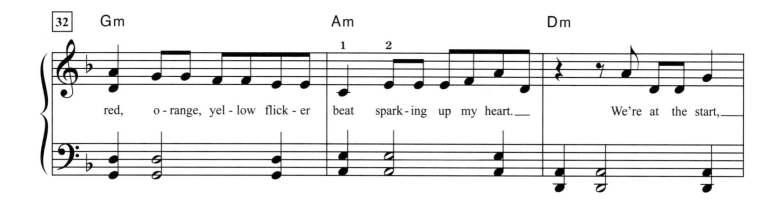

red, o - range, yel - low flick - er beat spark - ing up my heart.__ We're at the start,__

___ the col - ors dis - ap - pear, I nev - er watch the stars, there's so much down here,__

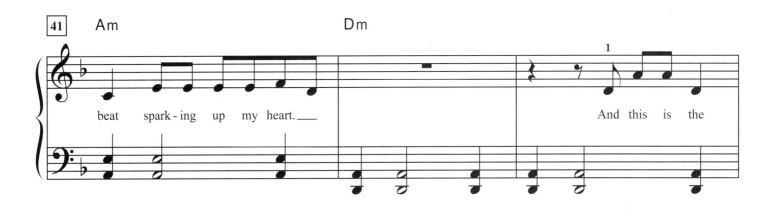

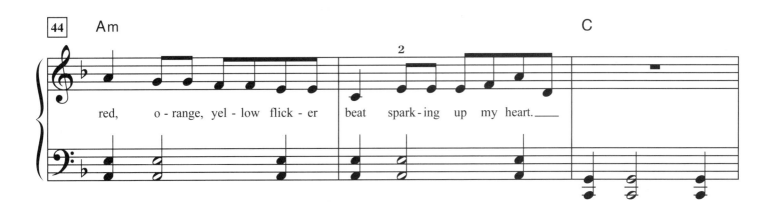

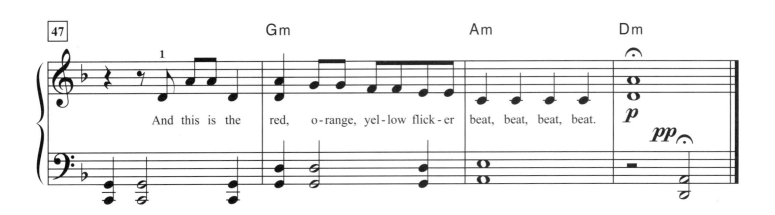

WHAT DO YOU MEAN

Words and Music by Mason Levy,
Justin Bieber and Jason Boyd
Arr. Albert Mendoza